MEXICO

by Joanna J. Robinson

The Child's World

Published by The Child's World®
1980 Lookout Drive • Mankato, MN 56003-1705
800-599-READ • www.childsworld.com

Acknowledgments
The Child's World®: Mary Berendes, Publishing Director
Red Line Editorial: Editorial direction
The Design Lab: Design
Amnet: Production

Design elements: Asaf Eliason/Shutterstock Images; Tony Baggett/iStock/Thinkstock; Gil C./Shutterstock Images
Photographs ©: Shutterstock Images, cover (right), 12, 13, 20, 28; Asaf Eliason/Shutterstock Images, cover (left center), 1 (bottom left), 16 (left); Tony Baggett/iStock/Thinkstock, cover (left bottom), 1 (bottom right); Gil C./Shutterstock Images, cover (left top), 1 (top), 16 (right); Hugo Brizard/Shutterstock Images, 5; Joanna Zaleska/Shutterstock Images, 6–7; Cristina Muraca/Shutterstock Images, 8; William Silver/Shutterstock Images, 9; Oksana Oliinyk/Shutterstock Images, 11; Stockbyte/Thinkstock, 14–15; Brian Florky/Shutterstock Images, 18; Steve Estvanik/Shutterstock Images, 21; Chad Zuber/Shutterstock Images, 22, 23; James Mattil/Shutterstock Images, 24; iStockphoto, 25; Danny Lehman/Corbis, 26–27; Anton Ivanov/Shutterstock Images, 30

ISBN 9781634070539
LCCN 2014959731

Printed in the United States of America
Mankato, MN
July, 2015
PA02268

ABOUT THE AUTHOR

Joanna J. Robinson is a creative educational writer. She has a passion for providing fun learning materials for children of all ages. Robinson has written educational content and more than 100 original stories. Trips to Mexico, Italy, England, Canada, and Egypt inspire Robinson to share her experiences with young readers.

TABLE OF CONTENTS

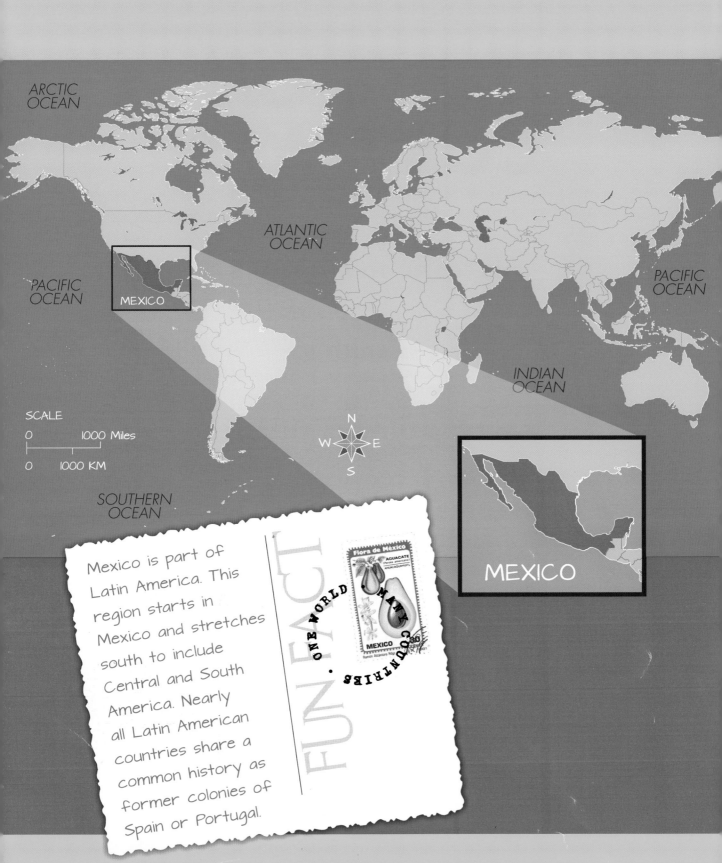

ARCTIC
OCEAN

ATLANTIC
OCEAN

PACIFIC
OCEAN

PACIFIC
OCEAN

MEXICO

INDIAN
OCEAN

SCALE

0   1000 Miles

0   1000 KM

SOUTHERN
OCEAN

N
W   E
S

MEXICO

Mexico is part of Latin America. This region starts in Mexico and stretches south to include Central and South America. Nearly all Latin American countries share a common history as former colonies of Spain or Portugal.

FUN FACT • ONE WORLD MANY COUNTRIES

Flora de México
AGUACATE
(Persea americana)
AHUACAQUAHUITL
MEXICO

CHAPTER 1

WELCOME TO MEXICO!

On November 1 and 2, Mexicans celebrate a special holiday. People of all ages wear skull masks. They dress in their fanciest clothes. They eat candy and cookies shaped like skeletons. They decorate the town with flowers, candles, and photos of dead relatives. It is Day of the Dead, *Día de los Muertos!*

↖ A woman dressed to celebrate
Día de los Muertos

On *Día de los Muertos*, Mexicans remember their dead relatives. They dance, sing, and make special altars. They have parades and parties. Families bring offerings to the dead. It is a way to honor them.

Día de los Muertos is just one small part of Mexico. It is a country of great variety. It has busy areas, such as Mexico City. It is one of the world's largest cities. Mexico also has quiet, sunny beaches.

Mexico's cities and beaches have made it a popular place for visitors. The natural beauty and rich culture have made Mexico a country unlike any other.

Many people visit Mexico to enjoy its natural beauty, such as the Misol-Ha waterfall in Chiapas.

CHAPTER 2

THE LAND

Mexico's coastline along the Yucatán Peninsula

Mexico is in North America. It is directly south of the United States. The two nations share a border. Mexico borders California, New Mexico, Arizona, and Texas. To the west is the Pacific Ocean. To the east is the Gulf of Mexico.

One part of Mexico is separated from the mainland. This land is called Baja California. It is south of the U.S. state of

California. The Gulf of California separates most of Baja from the rest of Mexico.

The Rio Grande is an important river in Mexico. It forms the border between Mexico and the United States. Each day, 2,000 workers cross the river. They legally enter the United States to work.

Most of northern Mexico is desert. Few plants grow there. The weather is hot and dry. The average temperature is between

The Rio Grande

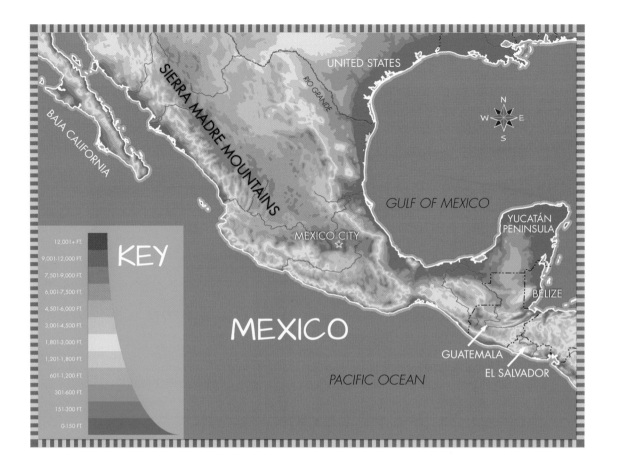

KEY

12,001+ FT.
9,001-12,000 FT.
7,501-9,000 FT.
6,001-7,500 FT.
4,501-6,000 FT.
3,001-4,500 FT.
1,801-3,000 FT.
1,201-1,800 FT.
601-1,200 FT.
301-600 FT.
151-300 FT.
0-150 FT.

UNITED STATES

RIO GRANDE

SIERRA MADRE MOUNTAINS

BAJA CALIFORNIA

MEXICO CITY

GULF OF MEXICO

YUCATÁN PENINSULA

BELIZE

MEXICO

GUATEMALA

EL SALVADOR

PACIFIC OCEAN

80 and 100 degrees Fahrenheit (27 and 38°C). The hottest months are July and August.

Central Mexico has mountains called the Sierra Madre. They cover about 75 percent of Mexico. Deer, coyotes, pumas, and rabbits live there. The weather in the mountains is pleasant. It is usually between 60 and 70 degrees Fahrenheit (18 to 24°C). Temperatures are much cooler on the highest peaks.

Southern Mexico has tropical rain forests. It is humid and hot there. The rainy season lasts from May to September. It rains for a few hours almost every evening. From June to

November, **hurricanes** are a danger. These storms strike the Yucatán and the Pacific coast.

Mexico's land has many natural resources. These include metals such as silver and gold. Rich soil is another resource. Farmers grow crops such as corn, wheat, and coffee. These crops are often sold to other countries.

Millions of monarch butterflies **migrate** to Mexico every year. They come from the United States and Canada. Some travel more than 2,500 miles (4,023 km)!

FUN FACT

ONE WORLD · MANY COUNTRIES

CHAPTER 3

GOVERNMENT AND CITIES

Popocatépetl Volcano rises above Mexico City. It last erupted in 2000 and thousands of people had to be evacuated.

Mexico's official name is the United Mexican States. It is home to 121 million people. The country has 31 states.

Downtown Mexico City has a large plaza called the Zócalo.

The capital of Mexico is Mexico City. It is a busy city. It is also one of the largest cities in the world. About 20.4 million people live within the city's more than 300 neighborhoods.

Many neighborhoods have small **plazas**. These open areas are places where people relax and visit with friends. Trees line the old stone streets. Old mansions stand in some neighborhoods. They have high walls and colorful gardens.

Mountains surround Mexico City. The mountains are beautiful, but they have also created a problem. They trap pollution in the city. Exhaust from cars and factories fill the air above the city. This air pollution hurts people's eyes and lungs. The city is working to fix this problem. Plants on rooftop gardens clean the air. People are encouraged to ride bicycles instead of drive.

Mexico City is also home to the nation's government. Mexico is a federal **republic**. The central government has some power. The states have

Some days the pollution in Mexico City is so bad that it is hard to see the mountains surrounding the city.

some power, too. The people elect officials who make laws. The states govern themselves and also follow national laws.

The president is the chief of state. He or she is also the head of the national government. Each president serves a six-year term. The president leads Mexico. The president also works with leaders of other countries. Leaders may talk about trading or how to solve world problems.

The country's leaders want to improve life for Mexican people. Mexico is a poor country. More than half of the people in the country live in **poverty**. That is about 52 million people.

It can be hard to find work in Mexico. People with jobs often earn low wages. Many work long hours. Sometimes families can only buy food and have no extra money.

Mexico's success depends on trade. It has **free-trade** agreements with many countries. Mexico often trades with the United States, Canada, and Spain.

Mexico **exports** many products. These products include fruits, vegetables, coffee, and tobacco. Mexico also exports clothing and cars. Other countries buy Mexican silver, too. Every year, about 70 percent of Mexico's exports go to the United States.

Mexico also **imports** goods. It buys products made in other countries. These goods include computers, phones, and

Mexico's currency

Mexico's flag

16

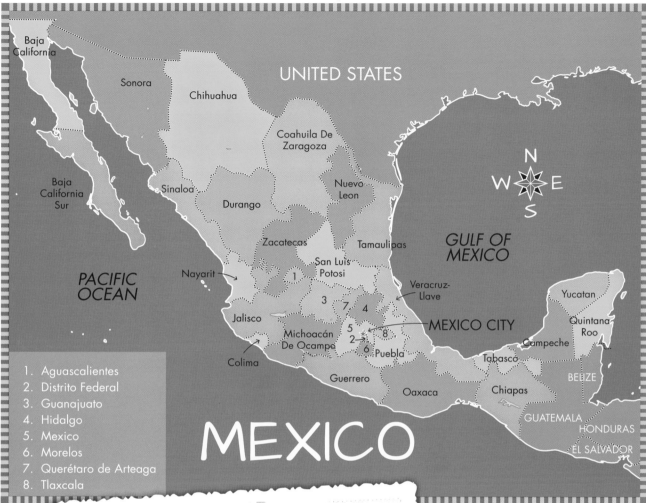

MEXICO

1. Aguascalientes
2. Distrito Federal
3. Guanajuato
4. Hidalgo
5. Mexico
6. Morelos
7. Querétaro de Arteaga
8. Tlaxcala

FUN FACT · ONE WORLD MANY COUNTRIES

Mexico City is built over the ruins of an Aztec city. The original city was on top of a lake. This land is marshy. The city is sinking 4 inches (10 cm) per year!

other machines. The United States and China are the biggest partners for these imports. Almost 50 percent of Mexico's imports come from the United States.

Mexico also makes money from tourism. There are many resorts and hotels in Mexico. People from other countries visit Mexico and use the hotels and restaurants. The money they spend improves the economy.

Mexico's beautiful beaches, such as this one in Cabo San Lucas, attract tourists from all over the world.

GLOBAL CONNECTIONS

Mexico and the United States share a border. It is easy for people to go from one country to another.

In 2013, more than 850,000 Americans moved to Mexico. Some people moved to start businesses. Others went to make a fresh start. Still others chose to retire in Mexico. Some stayed longer than expected. They did not have permission to stay longer. This made them illegal **immigrants**.

People also move from Mexico to the United States. Often, they are looking for work. Sometimes families move together. Other times children go alone. Parents send them to live with relatives in the United States. Some of the immigrants enter the United States illegally.

Both countries are trying to solve this problem. Patrols on both sides guard the border. More agents have been added at each border crossing. There are now water, horse, and bike patrols, too.

CHAPTER 4

PEOPLE AND CULTURES

↖ One way Mexicans honor their history is by performing traditional dances.

Before it was Mexico, the land was home to Mayans and Aztecs. Spain took control of the area around 1521. Mexico declared independence from Spain in 1810. As a result, Mexican culture is a mix of Mayan, Aztec, and Spanish cultures.

Most people in Mexico speak Spanish. Most Mexicans practice the Roman Catholic religion. Family is important to many Mexicans. Sometimes many generations share the same home.

Mexicans show pride in their country in many ways. They honor the Mexican flag by placing their right hands over their hearts to salute. People also celebrate national holidays, such as Independence Day. It marks Mexico's independence from Spain.

Mexico's national emblem, an eagle perched on a cactus, is lit up in honor of Independence Day.

Mexican Catholics walk toward the Basilica of Our Lady of Guadalupe in Mexico City as they carry her image.

Many Mexicans celebrate religious holidays. At Easter, people have processions. They perform plays about Easter. People go to Mass, which is a Catholic church service.

At Christmas, families often set up a nativity scene. They reenact the days before Jesus was born. People exchange gifts on January 6, the day the wise men brought gifts to Jesus.

Catholics also celebrate Our Lady of Guadalupe. They believe that in 1531, a man named Juan Diego had a vision. It was of Mary, the mother of Jesus. The Basilica of Our Lady of Guadalupe was built in her honor. On December 12, people visit it and make offerings to her.

Mexicans also celebrate *el Grito de Dolores*. This is Mexico's Independence Day, held on September 16 each year. People carry flags and shoot fireworks. The president rings a historic bell. The crowd shouts, "*¡Viva Mexico!*" It means, "Long live Mexico!"

Mexicans also celebrate birthdays. A *quinceañera* is a girl's 15th birthday. At this age, she is considered a woman. Her family hosts a big party. There is a special Mass to celebrate. Guests give the birthday girl gifts and jewelry.

FUN FACT · ONE WORLD · MANY COUNTRIES

The cocoa bean was first used in Mexico. The Aztecs crushed it and served it as a bitter drink. Later, Europeans added milk, vanilla, and sugar to it. Their additions turned the bitter drink into sweet hot chocolate.

CHAPTER 5

DAILY LIFE

Homes in San Miguel de Allende, Mexico

Many families live in small, simple houses. In the city, many people live in apartments. Often, three or more generations live together.

Families gather for a large meal at approximately 3:00 p.m. In some parts of Mexico, people take a nap after the meal. It is called a siesta.

Mexican families enjoy all kinds of entertainment. They listen to music and dance. Some people have hobbies such as sewing or painting. Many families enjoy visiting museums. Other families like watching sports such as soccer.

The tradition of cooking is important in Mexico. Mexican food is famous all over the world. Mexican meals include corn,

Some homes in Mexico are built into the sides of mountains.

beans, and squash. Tortillas, rice, avocados, chili peppers, tomatoes, potatoes, and lentils are also popular foods. Common fruits are papayas and plantains. For dessert, dulce de leche is popular. It is a caramel made from milk.

Mexicans wear clothes similar to those worn in the United States. For work, men wear casual pants and shirts. They may also wear coats and ties. Women wear casual pants or skirts with formal blouses. Young people wear T-shirts and jeans.

A woman waits for customers at her stall in a market. It is common to buy fruits and vegetables in open markets in Mexico.

Mexicans have many ways to get from place to place. People can walk or bike. In Mexico's cities, people take buses, cars, or taxis. In some cities, there are underground trains.

From busy cities to quiet towns, Mexico is a place with a unique culture and landscape. It has been shaped by its long history. Today, Mexicans are working hard to create a good future for their country.

Some people in Mexico enjoy wearing traditional clothing. This woman from Mérida, Mexico, proudly wears her colorful, handmade dress.

DAILY LIFE FOR CHILDREN

In Mexico, children attend school and do homework. They help with chores. Children play with friends. They spend time with their families.

A typical school day is four hours long. The school day begins with a salute to the flag. Children sing the national anthem. The day's lessons include Spanish language, math, science, and history. Children can learn a foreign language, such as English. Each day, students participate in art, gym, or religious activities. Between lessons, they have a *recreo*. This is a break from lessons. Children eat snacks and play outside.

Mexicans usually have two last names. A child is given family names from both their father and mother. This honors both parents.

FUN FACT

ONE WORLD · MANY COUNTRIES

Flora de México
AGUACATE
MEXICO

FAST FACTS

Population: 120 million

Area: 761,606 square miles (1,972,550 sq km)

Capital: Mexico City

Largest Cities: Mexico City, Ecatepec, and Guadalajara

Form of Government: Federal Republic

Language: Spanish

Trading Partners: The United States, Canada, and Spain

Major Holidays: Christmas, Easter, and *Día de los Muertos*

National Dish: *Mole Poblano* (a rich sauce made of chocolate, pepper, and spices that is often served over chicken or turkey)

Children in Mexico ride bicycles to get around their neighborhoods.

GLOSSARY

exports (ek-SPORTS) When a country exports goods, it is selling them to other countries. Mexico exports many products to the United States.

free trade (free TRAYD) Free trade is trade between nations without restrictions, such as high taxes. Mexico and the United States have a free-trade agreement.

hurricanes (HUR-uh-canes) Hurricanes are powerful storms with strong winds that can cause damage. Mexico's coast gets hurricanes.

immigrants (IM-uh-grunts) Immigrants are people who move to a foreign country to live. Mexico has many immigrants.

imports (ihm-PORTS) When a country imports goods, it buys them from other countries. Mexico imports many goods.

migrate (MY-grate) To migrate is to move from one place to another. Monarch butterflies migrate from the United States to Mexico in the winter.

plazas (PLA-zuhs) Plazas are open public areas with places to walk, sit, and shop. Mexico City has many plazas.

poverty (POV-ur-tee) Poverty is the state of being poor. Many families in Mexico live in poverty.

republic (ri-PUB-lik) A republic is a government in which people elect their leaders. Mexico's government is a federal republic.

TO LEARN MORE

BOOKS

Peppas, Lynn. *Cultural Traditions in Mexico.*
New York: Crabtree Publishing, 2012.

Petrillo, Valerie. *A Kid's Guide to Latino History: More than 50 Activities.* Chicago: Chicago Review Press, 2009.

Richardson, Adele. *My First Look At: Mexico.*
Mankato, MN: Creative Education, 2007.

WEB SITES

Visit our Web site for links about Mexico: **childsworld.com/links**

Note to Parents, Teachers, and Librarians: We routinely verify our Web links to make sure they are safe and active sites. So encourage your readers to check them out!

INDEX